ALL ASTURIAS

Text, lay-out and reproduction, entirely designed and created by the Technical Department of EDITORIAL ESCUDO DE ORO, S.A.

Photographs: F.I.S.A. in collaboration with Ediciones Alce.

1st Edition, November 1990

I.S.B.N. 84-378-1403-0

Dep. Legal B. 39280-1990

editorial **escudo de oro, s.a.** Palaudarias, 26 - 08004 Barcelona - Spain

Impreso en España - Printed in Spain
FISA - ESCUDO DE ORO, S.A. - Palaudarias, 26 - Barcelona (Spain)

Vista de Cobadonga.

An old engraving of a view of Covadonga.

The Cross of Victory, in the coat of arms of the Principality of Asturias, which legend says was brandished by Pelayo at Covadonga.

THE STARTING-POINT OF THE RECONQUEST OF SPAIN

Geography and history seem to have connived to make Asturias the redoubt where Pelayo held off the invading Muslims and from where the first victorious counter-offensives of the Reconquest were launched. ''To enter the spirit of Asturias'', wrote Ortega y Gasset, ''just as to enter its lands, a Castilian has to cross the mountain passes of the Cantabrian Cordillera. Leitariegos, Pajares, Piedrafita, Pontón, Pan de Ruedas! These, reader, are the passes, sublime, majestic locations of lofty solitude. They belong neither to León-Castilla, nor to Asturias, but are vantage-points from which you choose one or the other. From them, you behold on either side two contrasting landscapes which guard, like the sheath of a sword, two ways of life, two different and mutually opposing manners of saying *yes* to life.''

But even before Pelayo, the lands of Asturias had their claim on history. Prehistoric man roamed them, as is proven by the numerous remains discovered by researchers. From the Palaeolithic Age, findings from the Aurignacian, Solutrian, Magdalenian and Azilian periods have been made. Furthermore, in the caves of Penicial, Cueto de la Mina, Arnero, Ribadesella, la Franca, Buxu, Vidago and many more, evidence of the existence of settlements of fisherfolk, known as *Asturiense* has been unearthed. Interesting rock paintings dating back to this splendid prehistoric times are still to be seen in several of the caves of the region, such as those of Candamo, as well as the many megalithic monuments scattered over the Principality, the famous Peña Tú idol, the remains of the Celtic *castros* or fortified defences at Coaña and many skulls of prime importance in classifying the *crania hispanica*.

It is thanks to the might of the Roman Empire that Asturias entered into the pages of recorded history.

One of Oviedo's most important streets, Uría, and Escandelera Square by night.

The Asturians were finally defeated in 19 BC, after a long and desperate struggle, and were forced to abandon their encampments and their mountains, to settle in the valleys. In this way, Publius Carisio, first Roman prefect of *Asturias Trasmontana*, ensured that the warlike Asturians, with their profoundly independent spirit, would not attempt to rebel against his rule over their native lands. Of this period of Roman rule, we still have fine mosaics, such as those of Vega del Ciego, funeral inscriptions, those of Naranco or Cornellana among them, votive altars, coins and even features of present-day Asturian folklore, such as the Carnival-like celebrations of the "antruejo" or the "guirrios". But the most remarkable moment of the history of Asturias was when these lands became, with Pelayo and his followers, birthplace and symbol of the Reconquest against the Moors. A handful of Goth warriors led by Pelayo, having narrowly avoided annihilation at

the Battle of Guadalete, held out at Covadonga against the previously irresistible advance through the Iberian Peninsula of the Muslim armies. As a historically crucial consequence of Pelayo's successful resistance against the Arab troops at Covadonga, the Asturian monarchy quickly became a Christian stronghold which was not only a source of religious hope but which was also able to strengthen and unite, becoming the guiding force at the heart of the Reconquest. For a long period of time, the Church of Santa Cruz, built in Cangas de Onís on the site of an ancient dolmen during the reign of Favila, the son and successor to Pelayo who was killed by a bear, was the religious symbol and sacred place of the Asturians. The monarchy of Asturias continued from these early beginnings to be consolidated and to expand during the reigns of Alfonso I, Fruela I, Aurelio, Silo and their successors. Silo established his court in Pravia, and it was not until the reign of Alfonso I the Chaste that Oviedo became the capital of the kingdom.

The small lake, centrepiece of the gardens of the Campo de San Francisco.

OVIEDO

Founded in 761 on the hill named Ovetum, the city grew up around the San Vicente Monastery, which was built by Abbot Fromestano (or Frómista). Fruela I is thought to have been the first monarch to promote the growth of Oviedo. However, as Dolores Medio writes, ''It was Alfonso II who, transferring his residence to Oviedo, began to build up this tiny centre of population a few years later''. Alfonso ''encircled the village with strong walls, of which some traces still remain. He continued the rebuilding of several works which had been begun by his father after they had been destroyed or abandoned during the reigns of Silo, Mauregato and Bermudo I. He embellished the town with new buildings and churches, creating the first examples of what would later be known as pre-Romanesque Asturian art''.

Uría Street with the Campo de San Francisco gardens.

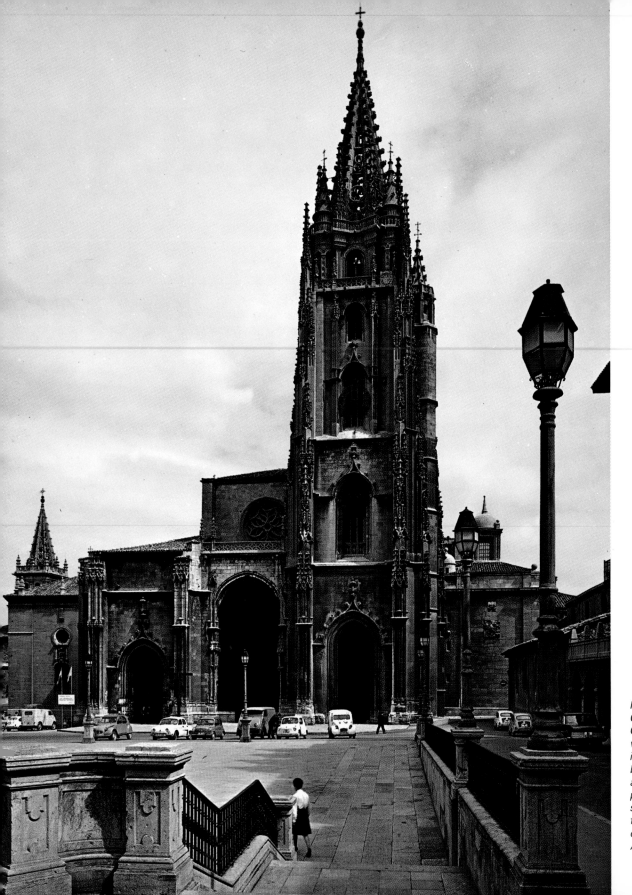

Front of
Oviedo
Cathedral
with its
impressive
bell tower,
a "romantic
poem in
stone", in
the words
of Leopoldo
Alas.

The cathedral cloister.

It is to Alfonso II that we owe such splendid works as the Cámara Santa, San Julián de los Prados (or Santullano) and Santa María de Bendones. Other kings also contributed to the making of Oviedo and patronised architecture in Asturias. Among these were Ramiro I, at whose command the churches of San Miguel de Liño, Santa María del Naranco, formerly a palace, and Santa Cristina in the district of Lena were built and Alfonso III the Great, who was responsible for the churches of Santo Adriano de Tuñón and San Salvador de Valdediós and the "Foncalada" fountain in Oviedo.

However, the until now ascendant star of Oviedo was dimmed when Alfonso IV transferred his court to León. Alfonso VI granted Oviedo the privileges and exemptions of a "Fuero municipal" and Alfonso VII accorded it the status of free city, but this did not prevent Oviedo from a long period of obscurity, almost anonimity. Notwithstanding, the city did play a role of some importance, particularly in the fields of religion and the arts, in the Middle Ages. It is significant that in the holy coffer, the Arca Santa, were deposited many treasures and relics in mediaeval times.

Some of the important events in the history of Oviedo are the building of the cathedral, which was begun in the 14th century, and the founding of the University in the 17th century.

Oviedo Cathedral: The 16th-century high altar, the work of Giralte de Bruselas and Juan de Valmaseda.

A detail of the high altar reredos, giving an idea of the richness of its decoration.

The Annunciation, one of the sculptures forming part of the high altar reredos.

Another of the sculptures decorating the high altar reredos, representing the Epiphany.

The Cross of Angels, donated by Alfonso II, the Chaste, in 808.

THE CATHEDRAL

Standing on the site of a church built by Fruela I in the 8th century and later destroyed by the Arabs and reconstructed by Alfonso II, the cathedral was built almost entirely in the 15th century, though begun in the 14th and completed in the 16th. It is a characteristically Flamboyant Gothic edifice consisting of a nave and two aisles, the largest of which is 67 metres in length, 10 metres wide and 20 metres high.

Its beautiful bell tower, the architectural pride of Oviedo, was defined "romantic poem in stone" by Leopoldo Alas and inspired this praise in the local dialect from Constantino Cabal, Chronicler of Asturias:

Mio torre: torrina de aguyes de piedra
qu'esguilen pel cielo lo mesmo que hiedra
coyendoi a mantes cachinos de tul...

The most remarkable features of the cathedral are the Churrigueresque Santa Bárbara Chapel, the early-16th century San Roque Chapel, the Chaste King's Chapel, with its Romanesque heads over the doorway, the Vigiles Chapel, the transept, containing ornate Baroque reredoses, and the magnificent reredos at the back of the high altar, considered one of the three most valuable works of its kind in Spain, along with those of Toledo and Seville.

The Cámara Santa is worthy of special mention. It is a jewel of Asturian Romanesque art, built by Alfonso II. Over this crypt is a barrel vault and the nave rises over three arches supported by six columns whose shafts are decorated with marble sculptures of the twelve apostles. The Arca Santa, or holy coffer, was covered in silver in 1075 and once held the important relics which are now on display: the Holy

The Cross of Angels, emblazoned in the coat of arms of Oviedo.

The 10th-century coffer known as the Arqueta de las Calcedonias, *given to the cathedral by Fruela II.*

Embossed silver chest, one of the many outstanding pieces in the cathedral treasury.

Shroud which is said to have been wrapped around Christ's head in the tomb, eight thorns from His crown, a piece of the cloth said to have covered Christ's body in the tomb, a piece of His robe, a small flask from Syria containing the blood shed miraculously by a crucifix and several fragments from the Cross of Christ.

Among the art treasures kept in the Cámara Santa are the Cross of the Angels, emblazoned with the coat of arms of Oviedo and granted to the cathedral by Alfonso II, the Cross of Victory, made of oak and

The entrance to the Cámara Santa.

covered with gold plate and inlayed with precious stones and enamelling, bestowed upon the cathedral by Alfonso III in 908, a 12th-century Romanesque diptych in silver and ivory, the *Cristo Nicodemus*, an 11th-century crucifix also made of silver and ivory, and many caskets, made of gold, silver and coral. The Gothic cloister is also remarkable, as are the archives, where codices and documents of such importance as the *Libro Becerro*, the *Libro de la Regla Colorada* and the Last Will of Alfonso II are kept, and the Diocesan Museum, which contains important archaeological remains from the 9th, 10th, 11th and 12th centuries.

The Cámara Santa in Oviedo Cathedral.

The ''Cristo Nicodemus'', an artistic crucifix made of silver and ivory to be seen in the Cámara Santa.

Cámara Santa: Byzantine diptych made of ivory, a priceless work of art.

The Arca Santa, donated by Alfonso III in 908.

The former palace which now houses the Town Hall. ▷

The coat of arms of Oviedo, in the Town Hall.

THE TOWN HALL

First built in 1622 and altered in 1780, the Town Hall (*ayuntamiento*) was then modified in 1881 and extended to in 1939. The building is a former palace whose original design is still preserved in its front. Its most interesting architectural feature is the large arch which once formed the Cimadevilla gate in the mediaeval city wall. At the side entrance, reached by walking through spacious porticoes, stands the stone statue of a lion, keeping watch over the stairway leading into the building.

The imposing Assembly Hall of Oviedo Town Hall.

Patio of the University of Oviedo.

THE UNIVERSITY

This vast, sturdy building of rectangular groundplan stands in the centre of Oviedo. Building on it began in 1534, when the institution was founded by Fernando Valdés, and was completed in 1608. Outstanding is the decoration of the fronts and the cloister, where there is a statue of the University's founder. The library, with its valuable collection of early printed books, *incunabula*, is interesting.

THE CITY

Oviedo is a city of great personality, both from an architectural and historical point of view and in terms of its people and culture. Clarín, in his splendid novel *La Regenta*, gives us a keen social description of the capital of Asturias: "Around the cathedral, occupying but little territory, stood what was formerly Vetusta (Oviedo), formed by what was once the Encimada (Cimadevilla) quarter, looking down on the

Plaza de la Escandalera, with the palace occupied by the regional autonomous government.

Detail of the front of the regional autonomous government building, formerly the "Diputación", or provincial administration.

Front of the Valdecarzaza Palace.

Front of the Campoamor Theatre.

town, which had spread out to the north-west and the south-east. From the tower could be seen, in the patios and gardens of old, ruined houses, remains of the old city wall, now used as party walls, amongst vegetable gardens and yards. Encimada was the high quarter and the poor quarter of Vetusta. The noblest and the most ragged lived there, the former in spacious ease, the latter huddled together''. The Oviedo described by Clarín still exists to a large extent, particularly around the cathedral. This part of the city contains streets such as Jovellanos, Azcárraga, Paraíso, Postigo Alto, Sol and Ramón y Cajal and the Mayor and Porlier squares, as well as a rich store of warm atmosphere and numerous fine old palaces offering profound insights into the history and architecture of Asturias.

But, there is, of course, another Oviedo, modern, dynamic and forward-looking, ceaselessly growing, expanding out in all directions, and in which the silhouettes of ultramodern edifices fill the gaze. The nerve-centres of this modern city are the Escandalera Square, the smart, busy Uría Street and the Campo de San Francisco. Calle Uría, with its shop-windows dazzlingly full of luxury goods and its smart cafés, is a street as elegant as any in a large city. The Gardens or Campo de San Francisco are the lungs of the city, a splendid green area covering some 60,000 square metres. It is a haven of peace, the resting-place of the city dwellers, with its charming alleys, the *paseos* de los Curas, del Bombé and de

The Camposagrado
Palace.

Front of the Hospice,
now converted into a
comfortable hotel.

Cloister of the Convent of San Vicente, now the Archaeological Museum.

los Alamos, its romantic small lake, where swans glide serenely, and the popular pavilion known as the *Escorialín*.

All aspects of life in the city of Oviedo are most pleasant. First of all, the food and drink of the area are excellent. The cider and the *Cabrales*, a cheese which has nothing to envy of the best French cheeses, are ample proof of this, and no less delicious is the succulent Asturian *fabada*. As the local saying goes, ''with beans and cider, we don't need petrol''. There are plenty of traditional bars and old-style taverns, always full to bursting with cheerful, friendly regulars, to be found in the city.

Sports-lovers will also find a wide range of activities available in Oviedo: the Tennis Club, the Royal Automobile Club and the Carlos Tartiere Stadium being just a few of the attractions. There are numerous cultural events in the city, too. For instance, the activities of the Capilla Polifónica Choir, the Cultural Club and the Association of the Friends of Nature, as well as the Opera season at the Campoamor Theatre.

The people of Asturias are experts in the art of combining their ''joie de vivre'' with a love of culture, and have also achieved a harmonious blend of tradition and progress in their lives and in their city. They have a healthy enjoyment of the present without forgetting their rich inheritance of glorious history. Not in vain does Oviedo's coat of arms feature the inscription: MOST NOBLE / MOST LOYAL / DISTINGUISHED AND UNVANQUISHED / HEROIC / AND FINE CITY / OVIEDO.

Oviedo Cathedral: the baroque of Santa Teresa.

Front of the Shrine of Cristo de las Cadenas.

The Rúa Palace, considered the oldest of Oviedo's many palaces.

A panoramic view of Oviedo, seen from Mount Naranco.

The pre-Romanesque Church of Santa María del Naranco.

MOUNT NARANCO

From the heights of Mount Naranco one commands splendid panoramic views of the city of Oviedo. The visit to the summer palace of Ramiro I and the Chapel of San Miguel de Liño is made even more rewarding by the fact that to get there the visitor has to take the Naranco road, and is thus obliged to follow the pre-Romanesque route.

The beginning of this route is reached by leaving Oviedo by Independencia, the street which is a continuation of Uría, then following Teniente Tejeiro until the street named after Ramiro I, at the end of which is the Avenue of the Monuments, (avenida de los Monumentos. An alternative route to the Avenue of the Monuments is via Independencia, Marquina Viaduct and Lago Enol Avenue. The road rises towards Mount Naranco, twisting and turning merrily between fields of rich green, running through the picturesque hamlets of the foothills. Though the mountain is steep, the climb is not difficult, and the marvellous views offered along the way make it an extremely pleasant excursion.

The visitor reaches the top of the mountain to be greeted by the sight of the whole Oviedo Valley, charming and rich in varied colour, laid out before him. This view becomes even more magnificent if he carries on up to the Aramo summits, from where one can admire the beautiful countryside as it stretches out towards the coast. The scenery to the north, with its thousand hues of green, is set off by the deep blue border of the Cantabrian Sea in the distance.

THE PALACE OF KING RAMIRO

Situated on the slope of Mount Naranco, some two and a half kilometres from Oviedo, this fine palace is without a doubt one of the most important pre-Romanesque monuments in Asturias. Left to oblivion for several centuries, it was declared a national monument in 1881 and restored, firstly in 1931, when the additional buildings defacing its authentic form were demolished, and after 1939. The construction belongs to the Ramiro, or Second pre-Romanesque Period, and its present layout consists of two rectangular floors, upper and lower. The vast chamber is powerfully attractive; it divided into three sections and covered with barrel vaults supported by transverse ribs. These arched ribs rest on side columns embedded into the walls and interlinked by round arches beautifully decorated with medallions and carved borders. More enchanting views of the surrounding countryside can be admired from the various view-points in the hall.

The lower storey, formerly a chapel, is covered by a barrel vault with two lunettes.

The palace was built in 848 and converted into a church in the 9th century, being known now as Santa María del Naranco.

A medallion carved in the stone walls of the Palace of Ramiro I.

The main hall of the Palace of Ramiro I.

SAN MIGUEL DE LIÑO

Just a few metres from the Palace of King Ramiro stands the Chapel of San Miguel de Liño, which belongs to the same period of pre-Romanesque art as its noble neighbour although its nave and aisles are separated by arches supported by columns which in turn rest on square bases adorned with primitive carvings of figures. The Byzantine influence can be seen in the capitals. Over the porch, there is a gallery with four openings formed by monolithic semicircular arches. Traces of wall paintings dating from the middle of the 9th century can still be seen on several of the walls and in the vaults of the nave and aisles. San Miguel de Liño was declared a national monu-

ment in 1885. On one of its walls, a human figure seated on a purple throne can be made out in the traces of decorative art remaining. The figure is seen in profile, but with face and arms facing to the front, and appears to be the portrait of a woman. Behind the throne, another figure, smaller and with arms and feet seen in profile, can just be perceived. According to the art expert Magín Berenguer, these figures form part of a scene depicting the Adoration of the Magi. There is also another figure, of similar characteristics to the two described above, on the east wall of the south nave. The yellow of the cloak worn by the figure and the purple background of the picture can still be appreciated.

San Miguel de Liño. In the foreground, the church bells, standing on supports built in 1970.

One of the beautiful windows in the Church of San Miguel de Liño.

Front of the Church of Santullano.

Rear-view of the Church of Santullano.

A view of the interior of the Church of Santullano.

Finely-decorated arches in the Church of Santullano.

A detail of the frescoes decorating the interior of the church.

SAN JULIAN DE LOS PRADOS

Also known as the Basilica of Santullano, San Julián de los Prados is the oldest and best-preserved pre-Romanesque monument in Asturias. The basilica consists of a nave and two aisles, which, like the transept, have wooden roofs. The rectangular sanctuary of the church contains three chapels covered by barrel vaults. An interesting and unusual feature of Santullano, which is also a national monument, is that the interior of the church is decorated in its entirety with splendid paintings. Outstanding amongst this profusion of artistic decoration is an ochre-coloured painting of the cross with the Greek letters alpha and omega adorning the arms.

Overall view of the Valgrande ski resort.

THE PAJARES PASS

Visitors entering the Principality of Asturias through the Pajares Pass are treated to an impressive visual experience as, suddenly, the monotonous landscape of Castile comes to an abrupt end, to be replaced by scenery of an astounding, awe-inspiring majesty. "To enter Asturias", in the words of Eugenio Nadal, "is to enter a solitary, isolated world. The vertical, inaccessible Pajares Pass: an immense amphitheatre of mountains with steeply-rising green slopes towering over dark valleys lost in the distance; a damp mist blurs the outline of the mountain sides, from where, from time to time, the peaceful, muted chime of a cowbell reaches the ear. Here, a waterfall crashes down with fresh, exuberant sound. Ahead, in the distance, the eye makes out red-roofed hamlets precariously perched on the steep foothills..."

Villages and hamlets pass by as the visitor penetrates the lands of Asturias. Valleys, mountains, woods and rivers, pastures and cultivated land are the features of this landscape until, suddenly, the mining valley is reached, after which the green of the Oviedo Valley, irrigated by the River Nalón, meets the gaze. As Ortega y Gasset writes in his travel book *Notas de ver y andar*, "(...) the first incautious glance we take from Pajares to the other side is always a failure. The eye loses its way a hundred times, waylaid by an enveloping substance like cotton: it is the mist, the lingering mist, rising in gusts like the deep breath of the valleys below".

Valgrande: the ski resort.

The Pajares pass.

The village of Pajares, and the pass.

Front of the Hermitage of Santa Cristina, Vega del Rey (District of Lena).

MIERES

Mieres is the capital of the mining valley watered by the Nalón and Caudal rivers, and is the most important city of Central Asturias. Its buildings are laid out in such a way that, as Victor Alperi says, ''(...) all its streets end in the mountains''. Socially and economically, the life of Mieres centres on the ''Fábrica'', the iron and steel works which has been the basis of the growth of the city since the middle of the last century. In more modern times, all the mines still active in the valley joined together to form the collective mining company HUNOSA.

COLLOTO

This pleasant village is situated on the main road between Oviedo and Santander. It is surrounded by beautiful countryside which becomes even more enchanting in the area around the River Nora. In Colloto itself, there is a fine 12-century Romanesque church, the Church of Santa Eulalia, whose most outstanding features are its triumphal arch and its capitals.

NOREÑA

This is village of ancient and noble ancestry — the bishops of Oviedo still retain the honorary title of counts of Noreña — grew up around its age-old castle and is now an important agricultural and industrial centre. Of its principal monuments, the most interesting are the palaces of Miraflores and Llanes or Rebollín, and the 17th-century church, which contains some excellent baroque reredoses.

View of the Jovellanos Park, in Mieres.

LA FELGUERA

La Felguera is an industrial and mining town separated from Sama by the River Nalón. The urban features of the town are strongly marked by its condition as a dynamic industrial centre, and by the passion for sports of all kinds of its inhabitants. The railway linking the Felguera Valley with Gijón has its origin in La Felguera. The writer Azorín, with his sharp eye, subtly captures the landscape with this description: ''And so night draws in; the train runs swiftly along the banks of the dark River Nalón, now and then rattling over an iron bridge; in the distance, the lights of a town glimmer...''

SAMA DE LANGREO

Like La Felguera, Sama is pre-eminently a mining town. Chief town of the district of Langreo, its economy is based on the mines of the area and on

Two views of the important mining town of Mieres.

La Felguera, a dynamic mining city.

coal-based industry. During the early years of the Asturian monarchy, Sama belonged to the crown. Later, Alfonso VI granted possession of the territory to the bishops of Oviedo, and it was finally restored to the crown by Philip II in 1575. Seven years later on, the district was granted independence as such.

RIOSECO AND THE RIVER NALON

There are several monuments of great interest to the visitor in the immediate vicinity of the small town of Ríoseco, amongst which we may mention the castle at Villamorey — in fact a mediaeval tower —, the Shrine of the Magdalena and the Church of Santa María. Around here, the waters of the River Nalón flow with more vigour and abound with trout. It is in this idyllic setting, nurtured by the waters of the river, that the action of Palacio Valdés's novel, *La aldea perdida* (The Lost Village), takes place.

INFIESTO

Numerous prehistoric and Roman remains have been discovered in this area, but it was not until mediaeval times that recorded history left its mark on Infiesto. It is now an enchanting town, surrounded by truly beautiful countryside, a dynamic agricultural centre which also has an important fish hatchery. Close to the town is the Shrine of the Virgin de la Cueva, a sanctuary formed by the hollow of a rock, and which inspired the popular verses which begin:

> *Que llueva, que llueva,*
> *oh, Virgen de la Cueva,*
> *Los pajaritos cantan,*
> *Las nubes se levantan...*

CANGAS DE ONIS

A town steeped in history, and where Pelayo set up his court after defeating the Arabs at the Battle of Covadonga. Cangas de Onís was the capital of the Asturian monarchy until this honour was transferred to San Martín del Rey Aurelio.

The town stands in the foothills of the Picos de Europa in a magnificent natural setting of magical beauty and charm. The streets of Cangas de Onís are graced by several fine old noble mansions. Entering the town, the visitor can admire the splendid bridge of Roman origin and which was altered in the 13th century.

The Buxu Cave, in Cardes, 2.5 kilometres from Cangas, is decorated with numerous engravings and paintings of animals and geometric motifs dating back to the Palaeolithic Age.

COVADONGA

According to legend, the Virgin Mary appeared before the Christian soldiers at the exact spot where the shrine now stands, and Pelayo, who was chosen as king on the same battlefield, received Her support. The name of Covadonga comes from *Cova-longa*, "Long Cave", and the legend also goes that the Virgin was already being worshipped here before the Muslim invasion of the Iberian Peninsula. The cave

Cangas de Onís: the "Roman bridge", as it is called.

Covadonga: monument to Don Pelayo.

The Basilica of Covadonga.

lies in the rocks high up in the mountains. Below it, a torrent rages down, its flow becoming more and more gentle as it joins the River Pozón then becomes a quiet brook. To the left of this mountain stream there is a spring which local tradition says bestows happiness and marriage on all those who drink of its waters.

The deeply venerated statue of the Virgin, an 18th-century carving affectionately known as the ''San-tina'', presides over the cave. The cave itself is reached by climbing up the more than one hundred steps leading to it, which many pilgrims ascend on their knees, or through a tunnel excavated in the rock, at the end of which are the tombs of Pelayo and Alfonso I.

At the foot of the cave is the Collegiate Church of San Fernando. Only the cloister remains of the original building. Construction of the modern basilica began in 1877, and it was inaugurated in 1901. The treasury forms part of the collections of the museum. The gifts offered to the Virgin include the magnificent crowns of the Virgin and of the Child. The polychrome wood statue of the ''Santina'', revered by the people of Asturias as ''their'' saint, owes its affectionate diminutive to its size, small in comparison to the norm in this type of statue. This is emphasized in a popular verse dedicated to the Virgin, which goes:

La Virgen de Covadonga
es pequeñina y galana.
Ni que bajara del cielo
el pintor que la pintara.

The Cave of the Virgin, Covadonga.

Large flocks of pilgrims visit Covadonga every year, not just from Asturias, but from all over Spain. The sheer, craggy, precipitous natural setting in which the shrine stands is extraordinarily, uniquely, beautiful.

On the esplanade of the basilica stand the seminary, the house of spiritual retreat, the chapter house, the modern lodgings of the canons, hotels for tourists and visitors and tourist information and post-office facilities.

In the centre of the square is an imposing statue by the sculptor Zaragoza of the daring Don Pelayo.

The Virgin of Covadonga, patron saint of Asturias.

THE PICOS DE EUROPA

This colossal mountain mass forms one of the most characteristic and beautiful features of the landscape of Asturias. Countless rivers and streams descend from the Picos de Europa to irrigate and fertilise the lower plains. The views in these mountains are unique, awe-inspiring in their tremendous beauty. The Picos de Europa form part of the Cantabrian Cordillera, extending over parts of the regions of Asturias, Santander and León. It was not until quite recently that the impressive rocks of their summits were trodden for the first time by the foot of Man. "Their beauty and splendour is such", says the Asturian writer Dolores Medio, "that the spirit is filled with awe and admiration when one contemplates these mountains. Words, adjectives, fail one. I would even say that they should not be described. They should be admired in religious silence, one should yield oneself up to the landscape. You have to feel like the eagle, and fly soaring upwards, leaving behind you, in the lower valleys, all the smallnesses of ordinary life, and climb up to the heights with your gaze fixed on the skies. The solitude, the infinite peace of the Picos de Europa, broken now and then by the sudden leaping of a chamois, refreshes the spirit, cleansing it with the cold, clear water of the mountain springs."

A group of mountaineers in the Picos de Europa.

The Picos de Europa are crowned by colossal rocks.

A view of the majestic central block of the Picos de Europa, the Naranjo de Bulnes Massif.

To get to the Picos de Europa, the visitor can take one of the routes which begin in the territory of Asturias itself, or from the neighbouring regions of Santander or León. The paths leading up to the peaks of these mountains are scattered with picturesque, delightful villages, each interesting in its own right. Among these villages are Arenas de Cabrales, Poncebos, and Panes, the chief town of the Peñamellera Baja district. Panes lies in the foothills of the Cuera Sierra by the side of the River Deva and is a paradise for hunters and fishermen. The Picos de Europa are formed by three massifs, the Andara, Urrieles and Cornión massifs, much of the area of which is contained in Asturian territory, and offer many and varied possibilities for the rest and relaxation of the visitor. One of the most beautiful and popular sightseeing routes begins at Covadonga, taking in the lakes of Enol before descending of the River Cares Valley down to Arenas de Cabrales. For mountaineers, the sides of Mount Naranjo de Bulnes, or Pico Urriellu, offer some of the most difficult and challenging climbs in the whole of Spain. For hunters, there is the Hunting Reserve of the Picos de Europa, and lovers of fishing will be delighted by the salmon and trout reserves of the rivers Sella, Cares and Deva.

The north face of Naranjo de Bulnes, 2,519 metres high.

An impressive close-up of the south face of Naranjo de Bulnes.

A view of the town of Llanes, with the clear blue of the Cantabrian Sea in the background.

Llanes seen from the sea, surrounded by fertile countryside.

PIMIANGO, COLOMBRES, VILLANUEVA...

This is a stretch of the coastline of Asturias in which prehistoric caves abound, among them the cave bearing the same name as that of the La Franca Beach, or that of Pindal, in Pimiango, in which there are splendid rock paintings. Nearby are the San Emeterio lighthouse, the Tina Mayor *ría* (estuary), and the ruins of the 12th-century Monastery of Santa Ana de Tina. Around Colombres, used as a resting-place by Charles I of Spain, and Villanueva, where the visitor may admire the magnificent Noriega Tower and several extremely interesting large, rambling old noble houses, the countryside is of exquisite and memorable beauty.

LLANES

The town of Llanes, enchanting and lovely, is the most important centre of population of Eastern Asturias. Many prehistoric remains have been discovered in the surrounding area. In mediaeval times, the district was known as "tierras de Aguila" — "lands of the eagle" — a term derived from Aguilar, the surname of the knights whose lands they were. The city was walled under the reign of Alfonso IX, who also granted Llanes its *Fuero*, or body of special laws and privileges.

Llanes contains a considerable wealth of monuments. Much of the mediaeval wall still remains, as well as a large number of buildings dating back to the same period and others erected in times of the Renaissance. The Parish Church of Santa María is very interesting. Built in the transitional style between Romanesque and Gothic, (between the 13th and 15th centuries), the church has a 12th-century front. Other outstanding monuments in Llanes are the house known as the Casa de las Sirenas, the Monastery of the Recollet Augustines and the house in Calle Mayor where Charles I stayed. Also recommended to the visitor is a walk around the picturesque, charmingly typical fishermen's quarter of the little town.

Not far from Llanes is the third airport of Asturias, the Cué aerodrome.

Llanes: the Church of Santa María.

A view of Sablón Beach, Llanes.

On the coast near Llanes is the rock known as the "profile of Christ".

The picturesque fishing port of Llanes.

Aerial view of Poo, a natural beauty-spot close to Llanes.

A panoramic view of Celorio.

The María Elena campsite, Celorio.

A pleasant view of the beach at Celorio.

Celorio's lovely beach.

Barro, a beach near the town of Llanes.

Lastres: the port, with the town in the background.

The Town Hall and Plaza del Generalísimo, Villaviciosa.

POSADA

An ideal starting-point to visit other attractive localities such as San Antolín de Bedón with its late Romanesque church, all that remains of the a 13th-century Benedictine monastery. Other picturesque villages in the vicinity include Niembro and Barro, two coastal resorts. The visitor will also find the delightful beach at Cuevas de Mar, the impressive monolithic monument of Peña-Tu and the caves of Bricia, Fonfría, Barro and Lledias, the latter decorated with various impressive rock paintings.

RIBADESELLA

Ribadesella is situated on the banks of the River Sella, famous for the international sports competitions which take place in its waters and for its abundance of salmon and trout. The town is divided into two halves by the river: the charming layout of the old town on one side, and on the other, the modern Ribadesella with hotels and cafés of more recent construction. A large bridge links the town with its magnificent beach. Ribadesella took on a certain importance in the mediaeval period, but the area was already inhabited in prehistoric times, as the remains found in the caves of San Antonio, Tito Bustillo, Las Pedrosas, El Cierro and La Cuevona clearly demonstrate. Pieces dating back to Roman times have also been discovered around of the town.

Among the monuments of outstanding interest in the town of Ribadesella are the various noble old houses which adorn its streets. Principal among these is the beautiful Renaissance palace of the Prieto-Cutre family. The international kayak race down the Sella, known more popularly as the ''Festival of the Canoes'', is an event during which the town really comes to life, the excitement and entertainment further increased by the presence of boisterous, exuberant groups performing popular dances and music.

The town of Villaviciosa seen in its beautiful natural setting.

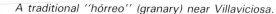

VILLAVICIOSA

The fourth town of the Costa Verde, Villaviciosa has been known by this name since the end of the 13th century. The Greek geographer Strabo mentions Villaviciosa's beautiful *ría* as the point marking the border between the *Asturica Transmontana* region and the territories of the Cantabrian tribes. The town is also referred to frequently, with various names — *Maliaio, Maiayo, Malayo* — in mediaeval documents. Numerous remains and findings, monuments and coins point to a possible Roman origin of the town. Villaviciosa was destroyed by a fire in the 15th century, and rebuilt thanks to the support of the Catholic Monarchs. It took on its noble place in history when Charles I of Spain landed at nearby Tazones.

The town of Villaviciosa is surrounded by marvellous countryside, and its praise is sung in the popular verse:

A view of Villaviciosa, surrounded by idyllic countryside.

Front of the Church of Santa María.

Villaviciosa hermosa,
qué llevas dentro
que me robas el alma
y el pensamiento.

The town is graced with many noble houses, and its most impressive monuments are the Church of Santa María, built in the transitional style between Romanesque and Gothic, the former Monastery of San Francisco, the monument to the apple by Benlliure and the house in which the Emperor Charles V stayed in 1517. In the surrounding district, the outstanding architectural works are the pre-Romanesque churches of San Salvador at Valdediós, San Salvador at Priesca and Santiago at Gobiendes and the Romanesque churches of Santa María at Valdediós and San Juan at Amandi, one kilometre from Villaviciosa.

The pre-Romanesque
Church of Valdediós,
surrounded by a superb
natural setting.

The Monastery of
Valdediós.

The village of Tazones,
with the port in the
foreground.

Dusk enhances the
charms of the port of
Tazones.

The San Lorenzo Beach, Gijón.

GIJON

This is the city of Asturias with the highest population and, sociologically, according to Juan Cueto Alas, whilst ''Oviedo is the administrative and cultural capital of the province in winter, this role is taken over by Gijón in the summer period, and not just due to the attractions of its beaches, but because, in the summer months, the people and the life of Asturias flee to the coast, and the city of Gijón rules the coast''.

Under Roman rule, that the city played an important role is borne out by the presence in the city of the Roman baths, and the first historical mention of Gijón in later times dates back to 857, the year when King Ordoño I made a donation to the city. After this,

Gijón is mentioned historically in relation with Alfonso III the Great, John I and Alfonso X, the Wise King. This coastal city supported Enrique de Trastámara, count of Gijón and Noreña, in his activities against King Peter the Cruel. It was delivered a powerful blow by history when the city was burnt down on the orders of the wife of Alfonso Enríquez to avoid its surrender to King Henry III, who, in turn, ordered it to be razed to the ground and taken over by the crown. It began to recover from the wounds of such a sad and terrible fate in the 15th century when the Catholic Monarchs approved the plan for the building of the port of Gijón. Three centuries later, Gijón was the capital of the Asturian seaboard, and was becoming an important industrial and commercial centre.

Part of the docks of
Gijón.

Aerial view of the docks
of Gijón.

Monument to the
Mother of the Emigrant,
facing the port of Gijón.

The port of Gijón by
night.

THE ROMAN BATHS

The Roman baths, which date back to the Ist century A.D., are situated at the foot of the Santa Catalina headland, exactly at the point known as the Campo Valdés. They consist of two buildings, occupying overall an area of 960 square metres. The best-preserved of the two buildings is the smaller one, with painted decoration on the friezes and socles. The baths were discovered in 1903.

THE CITY

Present-day Gijón has the air of a large, modern city, gaining its importance from tourism and industry. Despite this, the city still preserves its harmonious mixture of nobility and popularity, a fitting countenance for the charming birth-place of Jovellanos. Don Gaspar Melchor de Jovellanos, poet and politician and one of the city's most illustrious sons, as well as one of those who did most to make the city great, was born in Gijón, in the Cimadevilla quarter, in the middle of the 18th century.

The streets of Gijón are adorned with many fine old palaces, among them the Renaissance mansion which once belonged to the noble house of San Esteban, the Casa de las Recoletas and the Jove-Hevia family mansion. Of its religious buildings, we may mention here the Collegiate Church, built in

The Sailing Club, Gijón.

The San Lorenzo Beach,
which adjoins the city
itself.

The San Lorenzo
Promenade, Gijón.

The San Lorenzo Beach with the motorway in the foreground.

The mouth of the River Piles and the San Lorenzo Beach.

Another view of the San Lorenzo Beach.

1702 and later restored, and the chapels of San Lorenzo de Tierra and San Lorenzo de Mar. In the splendid Plaza Mayor, where one can while away many a pleasant hour under the porticoes around the square, stands the town hall.

In spite of the importance of the port, the dock still preserves its popular character, and harmonises with the town as an extension of the Cimadevilla quarter. The port facilities are excellent. Gijón has three industrial ports, Fomentín, Fomento and El Musel, and a fishing port.

The docks of Gijón, lively and popular, where one can visit the traditional old taverns and enter the con-

stant bustle of sailors, fishermen and shipping and transport workers, still remind one of the dynamic, vital atmosphere reflected by the Asturian novelist Armando Palacio Valdés in his work *La alegría del capitán Ribot.*

In the cultural life of Gijón, two institutions take pride of place. These are the Jovellanos Institute, founded by Gijón's illustrious son himself in 1794, and the Universidad Laboral, a splendidly-equipped college of advanced technology and agriculture, which occupies a huge, magnificent building decorated by artists of great renown.

The San Lorenzo Beach is the most popular and the

The monument to Don
Pelayo, standing before
the Revillagigedo Palace.

The picturesque
Cimadevilla quarter.

most beautiful of the beaches along the whole of the Costa Verde, a delightful festival of sand, sea and sun in the summer.

The Church of San Pedro stands on the very edge of the cliffs at the end of the Campo Valdés, the tiny promenade where the Roman baths are also to be found. This fine church was mentioned by Alfonso X in 1270, when he granted ''Our church in the city of Gijón which We ordered to be built in Asturias'', to the Monastery of San Vicente in Oviedo. Two years later, Alfonso emphasized in another document ''That all should worship at the church called San Pedro, which is in the possession of San Salvador in the city of Gijón''. The original church was razed to the ground by a terrible fire around the middle of the 14th century. In 1400, the city of Gijón, and with it the Church of San Pedro, were rebuilt by Royal Decree of King Henry III. The church was later further restored in the 16th, 18th and 19th centuries. It was destroyed again during the Spanish Civil War, and was once more rebuilt in 1945.

Another interesting monument to be seen along the promenade of the Campo Valdés is the palace of Don Fernando Valdés, which gave the promenade its name. Valdés was governor and life councillor of Oviedo and Gijón, lieutenant of Villaviciosa and quartermaster-sergeant of the Principality of Asturias. The Valdés Palace was built in the 17th century over the Roman walls formerly encircling the old city, occupying the site of the Tower of

The Plaza del Carmen, Gijón.

The Plaza del Humedal.

Augustus, a monument which was destroyed by fire. The magnificent palace features a pair of elegant towers decorated with Plateresque motifs. Adjoining it is the Chapel of the Virgen de Guadalupe, the architecture of which is in perfect harmony with that of the palace.

Campo Valdés forms a sort of antechamber to the charming Cimadevilla quarter. This is the quarter of the sea-faring folk of the city, an area of steep, peaceful streets, where Don Gaspar Melchor de Jovellanos was born. The 16th-century mansion where he first saw the light is situated in an enchanting square near to the Campo Valdés. The building, now the Jovellanos Institute, has been converted into a museum and teaching institution. Inside, books on the life and works of Jovellanos as well as manuscripts and objects related to this famous son of Asturias are kept. Some of the rooms of the building are dedicated to the history of Gijón, to mining and archaeology and to a newspaper soberby. Adjoining the Jovellanos Palace, archive elegant, in the same architectural style as the former, stands the Chapel of Nuestra Señora de los Remedios. In one of the side walls of this chapel, on the side of the Epistle, is the tomb of Jovellanos, which was designed by Juan Miguel Inclán. The epitaph to Jovellanos was composed by the 19th century poets Quintana and Juan Nicasio Gallego.

Aerial view of the Molinón football ground and sports complex.

Aerial view of the site
of the Asturias National
Trade Exhibition and the
''Pueblo de Asturias''
Ethnological Museum.

Another aerial view, this
time of the Gijón
camp-site.

*Part of the
Universidad
Laboral, or
College of
Advanced
Technology
and
Agriculture.*

Stained-glass window in the chapel of the Universidad Laboral, Gijón.

The central patio of the Universidad Laboral, Gijón.

Aerial view of Perlora.

The town of Candás with the port in the foreground.

A view of the beach at Candás.

Candás: the steps leading up to the Church of Cristo.

CANDAS

Candás is one of the main fishing villages of Asturias, and is also the centre of an important tinned foods industry. The village was the setting for the action of the novel *José* by Palacio Valdés.

This pretty village of the Costa Verde seems, like Narcissus, to contemplate its own reflection in the waters of the sea. One of the interesting monuments of the village is the Church of San Félix, which contains a baroque reredos with the so-called Christ of Candás. According to legend, this statue was discovered floating in waters off the coast of Ireland. In its honour, a popular celebration is held at the beginning of September. These ''fiestas'' are a favourable time for falling in love, as the popular song dedicated to them suggests:

> *Fui al Cristo y enamoréme,*
> *Malhaya la namorá.*
> *Fui al Cristo y enamoréme,*
> *Morena mía.*
> *No te podré olvidar,*
> *Malhaya la namorá.*

An aerial view of Candás.

The town of Luanco,
seen from the air.

Boats at the quay in
Luanco.

A view of the town of
Luanco.

Luanco: the port.

LUANCO

One of the seven towns of the Costa Verde, Luanco is the chief town of the district of Gozón. The town already existed in Roman times, and is now an important fishing port and summer holiday resort. Among the interesting monuments of the town, particularly fine are the parish church, which contains three priceless baroque reredoses, the Menéndez-Pola palace and the Sea Museum.

Front of the large, rambling Pola mansion, with its traditional eaves and balconies.

The promenade, Luanco.

The pretty port at
Luanco.

The beach at Luanco.

AVILES

The town of Avilés was already in existence in Roman times, and, in the old town, still preserves much of the urban structure and layout of the earlier periods of its rich history. It is now one of the densest and most important industrial centres of the whole of Spain, but even in mediaeval times it played an important historical role. Towards the end of the 11th century, King Alfonso VI granted the town a *Fuero*, which is kept now in the Municipal Archives. This special charter was confirmed by Alfonso VII at the end of the 12th century, and the Wise King granted Avilés new privileges and declared the town exempt from paying toll to the city of Oviedo.

In the old town, with its irregular pattern of steep, narrow streets, some of which are lined with porches, time seems to have gone so slowly as to have almost stood still. The monuments of this quarter include the Camposagrado Palace, whose front is emblazoned with a large coat of arms, the former Parish Church of San Nicolás, now the residence of Franciscan monks, with a front originally built in the 12th century, but since restored, and the Alas Chapel, a 14th-century structure. In the interior of the chapel, there are seven fine Gothic reliefs. To continue our description of the outstanding monuments of this quarter, there is the 15th-century house of the Baragañas, also known as the Palace of the Valdecarzana, and the Town Hall building, which stands on one side of Plaza de España. The front of the Town Hall is a noble work in the Herreran style, set off by a bell tower.

Plaza de España, or Plaza Mayor, "the main square",

The Church of San Francisco.

A panoramic view of Salinas Beach.

The port, Avilés.

is the nerve-centre of Avilés, where seven dynamic main streets have their origin. Some of these streets go down to the *ría* of Avilés, and it is these which are the most interesting and unusual. Other attractive streets are Suárez-Inclán, Pinar del Rio, formerly Ferrería, Alas and Ruíz Gómez, on one of the corners of which the Palacio Valdés Theatre stands. The first stone of this building was laid in 1900 by another of Asturias's illustrious sons, Leopoldo Alas.

The old town of Avilés within the walls contains the street of the Marqués de Teverga, which extends from Cámara street down to the edge of the *ría*. To the side of this street, we pass by the old market and Florida and Pedro Menéndez streets, leading down to the picturesque fishermen's quarter. Here, in General Zubillaga Street, we find the 12th-century Romanesque Church of Santo Tomás.

Of the modern Avilés, the great ENSIDESA Steel Centre deserves special mention as the driving force behind the town's industrial expansion. This industrial complex gave impulse to the modern-day development of this beautiful, dynamic town, and made a decisive contribution to the growth of population and industry. Other features of Avilés are its port, the Asturias airport, and the beaches of Arnao, El Cuerno and Santa María del Mar, on the coast of Avilés.

An aerial
view of
Avilés, with
the ría
cutting into
the
mainland.

Salinas, one of the most important summer resorts of Asturias.

The beach of Santa María del Mar, seen from the air.

EL PITO

Close to Cudillero, El Pito boasts the 19th-century Palace of the Selgas, which now holds an important museum. Among the treasures exhibited here are a number of frescoes, paintings by the great artists Goya and El Greco, and a superb collection of 16th-century tapestries.

PRAVIA

Pravia played an important historical role both during Roman times and in the mediaeval period. It is now an enchanting, prosperous town of noble streets and architecture, the centre of an important region in terms of farming and cattle raising. Of its monuments, the most outstanding are the parish church, once a collegiate church, the Moutas Palace, the Town Hall and the hermitage of the Virgen del Valle, built in the 14th century, in the interior of which there is a magnificent Renaissance altarpiece and a finely-carved polychrome statue of the Virgin. In the surrounding area, we find the village of Santianes, once the court of King Silo, with its splendid pre-Romanesque basilica and various rambling old noble houses, and, 12 kilometres from Pravia, San Román de Candamo. Here, there is the famous prehistoric cave, La Peña, and the fine 17th-century Palace of the Valdés Bazán family.

Luarca: the port.

Part of the city of Luarca.

The port of Luarca.

LUARCA

Luarca stands at the mouth of the River Negro, whose waters are rich in trout and eels, and which divides the town into two unequal parts, connected by seven bridges. A town of whitewashed houses and enchanting layout, Luarca is one of the most beautiful of the coastal cities of Asturias, its attraction to tourists heightened even more by the proximity of three magnificent beaches.

Of its various monuments, the most outstanding are the parish church, the 14th-century Palace of the Marquis of Ferrera, the Gamoneda House, which dates back to the 18th century and the building formerly occupied by the town hall. A pleasant visit can also be made to the attractive, charming Pescadería and Cambaral quarters of the town.

The sheltered port of Luarca, seen from the air.

According to local tradition, the name of the latter quarter comes from the pirate Kamboral, said to have slain the nobleman Don Teudo de Villademoros. Another legend tells the story of the frequent, devastating sea-raids of the Normans in the mid-9th century. The Cambaral quarter of the present day is a delightful, picturesque part of the town. One gets there by taking the street of the same name, which leads out to the Atalaya headland. In Cambaral, we find the Plaza de la Mesa, a square where, from the mediaeval times, the town council gathered round it and later the "Noble Guild of Sea-farers and Navigators", where discussions took place on sub-

jects of concern to the guilds, such as the shortage of salt, the annual projects of the whaling community or the content of the old Royal Decrees requesting support in fighting heresy or the Moors.

In the Cambaral quarter stands a monument representing and commemorating fourteen important events in the history of Luarca.

Also of outstanding interest is the popular hermitage of the Blanca, which stands near to the cemetery. This shrine was built in honour of the Virgin who, according to traditional lore, appeared in the Cave of the Blanca in November 1530.

The city of Luarca by night.

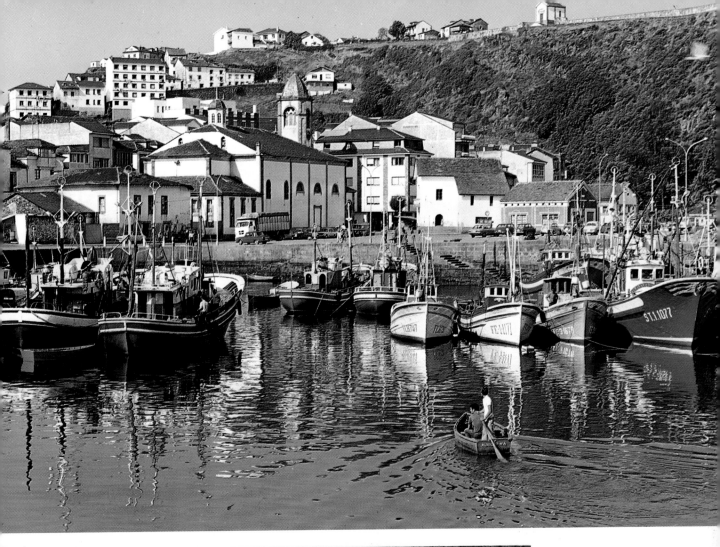

Another view of the
port of Luarca.

The Town Hall, standing
in the Plaza del
Ayuntamiento.

Part of the town of Navia.

NAVIA

Navia is situated at the estuary of the River Navia, whose origins are described by Camilo José Cela: ''Up there where men live, and love, and govern themselves and die as they did at the beginning of time, up there in the age-old lands of Lugo, on the ancient Mount Cebrero, a bubbling, childlike Navia is born, which grows and expands through Navia de Suarna and the sierras of Busto, through Piedras Apañadas and San Roque, descending to water, Navia...'' The origins of Navia go back, it is thought, to Roman times, and the town played a modest but significant role during the mediaeval period. Several palaces and houses still remain to bear witness to Navia's noble past.

The River Navia, at whose mouth stands the town of the same name.

Ruins of a Celtic settlement, Coaña.

Overall view of Tapia de Casariego.

Tapia de Casariego,
seen from the air.

A view of the port of
Tapia de Casariego.

Figueras.

CASTROPOL

Perched on the top of a promontory looking out over the waters of the beautiful *ría* of the River Eo to the lands of Galicia on the other side, Castropol has the structure of a castle or watchtower. With its historic old palaces, its solitary little squares and its white houses with their slate roofs, Castropol is one of the most attractive of all the towns of Asturias, attractive in its silence and peacefulness. It is like a marvellous balcony hanging out over the *ría*. Of its architectural beauties, the most interesting are the Chapel of Nuestra Señora del Campo, built in the 15th century, the Church of Santiago and the splendid Montenegro and Valledor palaces.

A number of memorable excursions can be made from Castropol. Places to visit include Vegadeo, situated at the beginning of the *ría*, at the other end of which, opposite Castropol, stands the Galician village of Ribadeo. Recommended also are Villanueva de los Oscos, Tapia de Casariego, Santa María de los Oscos and Santa Eulalia de los Oscos, where the Marquis of Sargadelos was born. Towards the end of the 18th century, this nobleman founded the famous chinaware factory bearing his name.

Part of the town of Castropol, with the "ría" in the background.

CANGAS DE NARCEA

That the Romans settled here for at least a time is demonstrated by the primitive kilns, coins and other remains found in the vicinity of Cangas de Narcea. This attractive town boasts several old palaces such as that of the Queipo de Llano family, now the town hall, and the 16th-century Omaña Palace. The religious architecture of the town includes the Church of Santa María Magdalena, which dates back to the 17th century, and the Monastery at Corias, popularly known as the ''Escorial of Asturias''.

TINEO

This town is situated in the foothills of the Tineo Sierra, and is surrounded by idyllic countryside. Tineo has a noble, aristocratic air, given to it by the charming, irregular pattern of its pleasant streets and the presence of several monuments of great artistic and architectural value. These include the 13th-century Parish Church, built in the transitional style between Romanesque and Gothic, the beautiful Gothic palace of the Maldonado and Campomanes families, the Meras mansion and the former pilgrims' hospital, which still contains traces of mediaeval paintings. Of modern Tineo, the most attractive aspect is its many taverns and restaurants, where the delicious delicacies of the region, its famous ham, salmon and trout dishes, are recommended.

GRADO

This town stands on the site of the old Roman settlement, and had a history of ups and downs in the Middle Ages. Remains of castles, palaces and noble mansions bear witness to the past splendour of the town. Not far from Grado is the Romanesque Church of Santa Eulalia, dating back to the 12th century, where Bishop Adulfo is buried, and the Romanesque Church of San Martín de Gurullés, also 12th century, and the mediaeval Coalla Tower.

Castropol: monument to Villaamil.

GASTRONOMY

Asturias is a region of excellent food and drink, offering an unequalled variety of exquisite dishes. Among these, pride of place goes to the famous *fabada*, and its most popular variant, Asturian *pote*. Then there are *arbeyos* (peas) with ham and a wide range of delicious soups, and the succulent *caldereta* (fish stew), and an infinity of fish dishes: hake ''a la sidra'' or ''a la antigua'', served with asparagus tips and green beans, bream, sardines, trout, salmon and many more, as well as all the different types of seafood imaginable. A meat dish which is strongly recommended is the *estofado de buey* (ox stew), prepared with veal foot, bacon, onions, turnip, herbs, pepper and wine.

For dessert, any Asturian cheese, but particularly *Cabrales* (''blue'' ewes' milk cheese), or one of the local sweet delicacies, *casadielles* or *arroz con leche*, a rice pudding which has its origins precisely here, in Asturias.

To drink, one must try the deliciously refreshing, slightly sour-tasting, digestive local cider, the celebrated popular beverage of Asturias.

One of the most popular dishes in the whole of Spain, the succulent Asturian ''fabada''.

THE FOLKLORE OF ASTURIAS

Asturian folklore is one of the richest, oldest and most attractive of all the regions of Spain. The *corri-corri* is perhaps the oldest of the local dances. It is a ritual dance of prehistoric roots, originally performed in Cabrales. In its modern form, it is danced by six women and a man, who simulate the eternal rites of love in their leaping and dodging. Other dances of age-old antiquity are the *pericote*, the *danza prima* and the traditional dances of the cowherds, all danced to the accompaniment of the *payecha*, a type of pan which is struck with an enormous key. The bagpipes and the small drum are, as in neighbouring Galicia, the most deeply-rooted musical instruments of the region. A popular festival is that of the cowherds of the mountain pastures in Aristébano (between the districts of Luarca and Tineo). The most spectacular event during these festivities is the celebration of a cowherds' wedding, which is accompanied by wedding songs:

> *Aqui van lus de la boda*
> *todus llevan vestíu negru*
> *menos la señora novia,*
> *que viene de terciopelo.*

After the ceremony, there is dancing and the singing of traditional songs of the cowherds, and the festivities end with a meal in the open air.

Among the traditional *fiestas* of Asturias, the most interesting are the typical *romería* (festival at a local shrine) to the statue of Christ, protector of Candás, the ''festival of the shepherd'' at Covadonga, the lively *romerías* at Grado, the ''fiesta de los huevos pintos'',artistically-decorated eggs sold at Easter, the *romería del Carmín* in Pola de Siero, the ''fiesta'' of Saint Matthew in Oviedo and the festivities of the Assumption in Gijón.

The art of pouring cider, the typical drink of Asturias.

Asturians dressed in the traditional costumes of the region.

Contents

THE STARTING-POINT OF THE
  RECONQUEST OF SPAIN 2
OVIEDO 5
THE CATHEDRAL 10
THE TOWN HALL 14
THE UNIVERSITY 16
THE CITY 16
MOUNT NARANCO 22
THE PALACE OF KING RAMIRO 24
SAN MIGUEL DE LIÑO 26
SAN JULIAN DE LOS PRADOS 29
THE PAJARES PASS 30
MIERES 33
COLLOTO 33
NOREÑA 33
LA FELGUERA 34
SAMA DE LANGREO 34
RIOSECO AND THE RIVER NALON 35
INFIESTO 35
CANGAS DE ONIS 36
COVADONGA 36

THE PICOS DE EUROPA 40
PIMIANGO, COLOMBRES,
  VILLANUEVA 45
LLANES 45
POSADA 51
RIBADESELLA 51
VILLAVICIOSA 52
GIJON 56
THE ROMAN BATHS 59
THE CITY 59
CANDAS 71
LUANCO 74
AVILES 77
EL PITO 81
PRAVIA 81
LUARCA 82
NAVIA 86
CASTROPOL 90
CANGAS DE NARCEA 91
TINEO 91
GRADO 91
GASTRONOMY 92
THE FOLKLORE OF ASTURIAS 93

Collection ALL EUROPE

	Spanish	French	English	German	Italian	Catalan	Dutch	Swedish	Portuguese	Japanese	Finnish
1 ANDORRA	•	•	•	•	•	•					
2 LISBON	•	•	•	•	•				•		
3 LONDON	•	•	•	•	•						
4 BRUGES	•	•	•	•	•		•				
5 PARIS	•	•	•	•	•					•	
6 MONACO	•	•	•	•	•						
7 VIENNA	•	•	•	•	•			•		•	
8 NICE	•	•	•	•	•						
9 CANNES	•	•	•	•							
10 ROUSSILLON	•	•	•	•			•				
11 VERDUN	•	•	•	•			•				
12 THE TOWER OF LONDON	•	•	•								
13 ANTWERP	•	•	•	•							
14 WESTMINSTER ABBEY	•	•	•								
15 THE SPANISH RIDING SCHOOL IN VIENNA	•	•	•	•							
16 FATIMA	•	•	•	•	•			•			
17 WINDSOR CASTLE	•	•	•	•	•					•	
18 THE OPAL COAST	•	•									
19 COTE D'AZUR	•	•	•	•							
20 AUSTRIA	•	•	•	•							

Currently being prepared

	Spanish	French	English	German	Italian	Catalan	Dutch	Swedish	Portuguese	Japanese	Finnish
21 LOURDES	•	•	•	•	•		•				
22 BRUSSELS	•	•	•	•	•						
23 SCHÖNBRUNN PALACE	•	•	•	•	•			•			
24 ROUTE OF PORT WINE	•	•	•	•	•				•		
25 CYPRUS	•	•	•	•							
26 HOFBURG PALACE	•	•	•	•	•						
27 ALSACE	•	•	•	•	•		•				
28 RHODES	•	•	•								

Currently being prepared

	Spanish	French	English	German	Italian	Catalan	Dutch	Swedish	Portuguese	Japanese	Finnish
29 BERLIN											
30 CORFU		•	•	•							
31 MALTA		•	•	•							
32 PERPIGNAN		•									
33 STRASBOURG	•	•	•	•	•						

Currently being prepared

	Spanish	French	English	German	Italian	Catalan	Dutch	Swedish	Portuguese	Japanese	Finnish
34 MADEIRA											
35 CERDAGNE - CAPCIR				•							

Currently being prepared

	Spanish	French	English	German	Italian	Catalan	Dutch	Swedish	Portuguese	Japanese	Finnish
36 CARCASSONE											

Currently being prepared

37 AVIGNON

Collection ART IN SPAIN

Now being revised

	Spanish	French	English	German	Italian	Catalan	Dutch	Swedish	Portuguese	Japanese	Finnish
1 PALAU DE LA MUSICA CATALANA (Catalan Palace of Music)											
2 GAUDI	•	•	•	•	•					•	
3 PRADO MUSEUM I (Spanish Painting)	•	•	•	•	•					•	
4 PRADO MUSEUM II (Foreign Painting)	•	•	•	•	•						
5 MONASTERY OF GUADALUPE	•										
6 THE CASTLE OF XAVIER	•	•	•	•						•	
7 THE FINE ARTS MUSEUM OF SEVILLE	•	•	•	•	•						
8 SPANISH CASTLES	•	•	•	•							
9 THE CATHEDRALS OF SPAIN	•	•	•	•							
10 THE CATHEDRAL OF GERONA	•	•	•	•							
11 GRAN TEATRE DEL LICEU DE BARCELONA (The Great Opera House)											

Now being revised
Currently being prepared

	Spanish	French	English	German	Italian	Catalan	Dutch	Swedish	Portuguese	Japanese	Finnish
12 THE ROMANESQUE STYLE IN CATALONIA	•	•	•	•							
13 LA RIOJA: ART TREASURES AND WINE-GROWING RESOURCES	•	•	•	•							
14 PICASSO	•	•	•	•						•	
15 REALES ALCAZARES (ROYAL PALACE OF SEVILLE)	•	•	•	•							
16 MADRID'S ROYAL PALACE	•	•	•	•							
17 ROYAL MONASTERY OF EL ESCORIAL	•	•	•	•							
18 THE WINES OF CATALONIA	•	•	•	•							
19 THE ALHAMBRA AND THE GENERALIFE	•	•	•	•							
20 GRANADA AND THE ALHAMBRA (ARAB AND MAURESQUE MONUMENTS OF CORDOVA, SEVILLE AND GRANADA)	•										
21 ROYAL ESTATE OF ARANJUEZ	•	•	•	•							
22 ROYAL ESTATE OF EL PARDO	•	•	•	•							
23 ROYAL HOUSES	•	•	•	•							
24 ROYAL PALACE OF SAN ILDEFONSO	•	•	•	•							
25 HOLY CROSS OF THE VALLE DE LOS CAIDOS	•	•	•	•							
26 OUR LADY OF THE PILLAR OF SARAGOSSA	•	•	•	•							

Currently being prepared

27 MORELLA

Collection ALL SPAIN

	Spanish	French	English	German	Italian	Catalan	Dutch	Swedish	Portuguese	Japanese	Finnish
1 ALL MADRID	•	•	•	•	•					•	
2 ALL BARCELONA	•	•	•	•	•	•					
3 ALL SEVILLE	•	•	•	•	•					•	
4 ALL MAJORCA	•	•	•	•	•						
5 ALL THE COSTA BRAVA	•	•	•	•	•						
6 ALL MALAGA and the Costa del Sol	•	•	•	•	•		•				
7 ALL THE CANARY ISLANDS, Gran Canaria, Lanzarote and Fuerteventura	•	•	•	•	•		•	•			
8 ALL CORDOBA	•	•	•	•	•					•	
9 ALL GRANADA	•	•	•	•	•					•	
10 ALL VALENCIA	•	•	•	•	•						
11 ALL TOLEDO	•	•	•	•	•					•	
12 ALL SANTIAGO	•	•	•	•	•						
13 ALL IBIZA and Formentera	•	•	•	•	•						
14 ALL CADIZ and the Costa de la Luz	•	•	•	•	•						
15 ALL MONTSERRAT	•	•	•	•	•	•					
16 ALL SANTANDER and Cantabria	•		•								
17 ALL THE CANARY ISLANDS II, Tenerife, La Palma, Gomera, Hierro	•	•	•	•	•		•	•			

Currently being prepared

18 ALL ZAMORA

Currently being prepared

19 ALL PALENCIA

	Spanish	French	English	German	Italian	Catalan	Dutch	Swedish	Portuguese	Japanese	Finnish
20 ALL BURGOS, Covarrubias and Santo Domingo de Silos	•	•	•	•	•						
21 ALL ALICANTE and the Costa Blanca	•	•	•	•	•						
22 ALL NAVARRA	•	•	•	•	•						
23 ALL LERIDA, Province and Pyrenees	•	•	•	•		•					
24 ALL SEGOVIA and Province	•	•	•	•							
25 ALL SARAGOSSA and Province	•	•	•	•					•		
26 ALL SALAMANCA and Province	•	•	•	•						•	
27 ALL AVILA and Province	•	•	•	•							
28 ALL MINORCA	•	•	•	•							
29 ALL SAN SEBASTIAN and Guipúzcoa	•										
30 ALL ASTURIAS	•	•	•	•							
31 ALL LA CORUNNA and the Rías Altas	•	•	•	•							
32 ALL TARRAGONA and Province	•	•	•	•							
33 ALL MURCIA and Province	•	•	•	•							
34 ALL VALLADOLID and Province	•	•	•	•							
35 ALL GIRONA and Province	•	•	•	•							
36 ALL HUESCA and Province	•	•									
37 ALL JAEN and Province	•	•	•	•							
38 ALL ALMERIA and Province	•	•	•								

Currently being prepared

	Spanish	French	English	German	Italian	Catalan	Dutch	Swedish	Portuguese	Japanese	Finnish
39 ALL CASTELLON and the Costa del Azahar	•	•	•	•							
40 ALL CUENCA and Province	•	•	•	•							
41 ALL LEON and Province	•	•	•	•							
42 ALL PONTEVEDRA, VIGO and the Rías Bajas	•	•	•	•							
43 ALL RONDA	•	•	•	•							
44 ALL SORIA	•										

Currently being prepared

	Spanish	French	English	German	Italian	Catalan	Dutch	Swedish	Portuguese	Japanese	Finnish
45 ALL HUELVA											
46 ALL EXTREMADURA	•										
47 ALL ANDALUSIA											

Currently being prepared

48 ALL GALICIA
Currently being prepared

49 ALL CATALONIA
Currently being prepared

50 ALL LA RIOJA
Currently being prepared

51 ALL LUGO

Collection ALL AMERICA

	Spanish	French	English	German	Italian	Catalan	Dutch	Swedish	Portuguese	Japanese	Finnish
1 PUERTO RICO	•		•								
2 SANTO DOMINGO	•		•								
3 QUEBEC			•	•							
4 COSTA RICA	•		•								

Collection ALL AFRICA

	Spanish	French	English	German	Italian	Catalan	Dutch	Swedish	Portuguese	Japanese	Finnish
1 MOROCCO	•	•	•	•	•						
2 THE SOUTH OF MOROCCO	•	•	•	•	•						
3 TUNISIA		•	•	•	•						

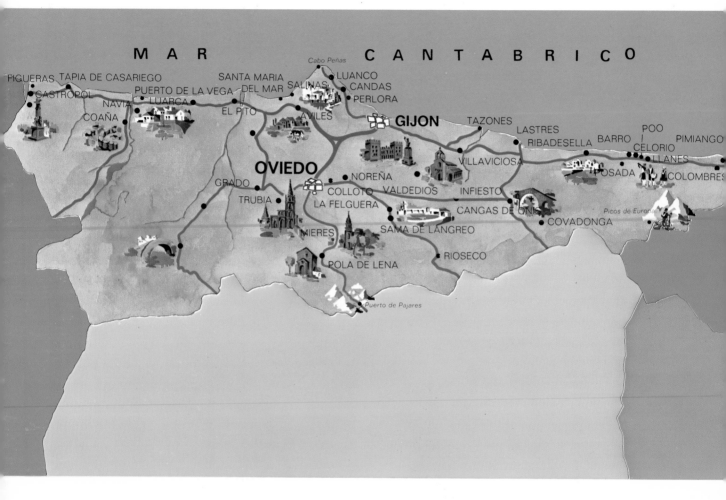

MAR CANTABRICO

Cabo Peñas

FIGUERAS TAPIA DE CASARIEGO SANTA MARIA SALINAS LUANCO CANDAS
CASTROPOL PUERTO DE LA VEGA DEL MAR PERLORA
NAVIA LUARCA TAZONES
COAÑA EL PITO AVILES GIJON LASTRES POO PIMIANGO
BARRO CELORIO LLANES
OVIEDO VILLAVICIOSA RIBADESELLA POSADA COLOMBRES
GRADO NOREÑA VALDEDIOS INFIESTO
TRUBIA COLLOTO CANGAS DE ONIS Picos de Europa
LA FELGUERA COVADONGA
MIERES SAMA DE LANGREO
POLA DE LENA RIOSECO

Puerto de Pajares

FRANCIA

PORTUGAL

ISLAS BALEARES

ISLAS CANARIAS

The printing of this book was completed
in the workshops of
FISA - ESCUDO DE ORO, S.A.
Palaudarias, 26 - Barcelona (Spain)